Joy is a
Choice
Choose Joy!
Jordan McCulloy

PRAISE FOR
Kathy Said, You're Not Lost to Me

"This is a gem of a book. It speaks of real life drama, of personal anguish and then grateful healing and recovery. It is one more testament to the courage of the individual, the message of the Twelve-Step Program, and the wisdom of a committed therapist. The section on the interaction of the therapist and the patient is particularly well done. I highly recommend it."

—JACK MCINTYRE, PAST PRESIDENT, AMERICAN PSYCHIATRIC ASSOCIATION

"This book is clear, concise, insightful and real. An impossible journey well traveled."

—DR. E.A. SEARS, PRESIDENT, WORKPLACE COMMUNICATIONS

"Concisely and powerfully written, *Kathy Said, You're Not Lost to Me* is an emotionally moving and genuine account of one remarkable woman's journey through pain and healing. Poignant and truthfully inspired, this book is a real gift."

—LAURIE WOODFORD, PROFESSOR AND TRAVEL WRITER

"This book is a demonstration of the phenomenal strength and healing ability of the human spirit. This story must be shared."

—JILL FORTUNE, RETIRED SOCIAL WORKER AND
AUTHOR OF *DREAMS LIKE BLUE MORNING GLORIES*

"This book is clear, easy to read and understand, and gives "life jewels" to hold on to, to give one courage and hope.What a gift for anyone struggling for answers and needs 'easy.'"

—RAE FOSTER, SPIRITUAL TEACHER

Kathy Said,
You're Not Lost to Me

Jackie McCullough

JOY
CHOICE
PRESS

Printed in the United States of America

ISBN-13: 978-1490442587
ISBN-10: 1490442588

Joy Choice Press
JoyChoice.net

DEDICATION

THIS BOOK IS DEDICATED to Kathy Martin, LCSW, my therapist for thirteen years; Joan Cook, my trusted friend who was my daily confidant, listener, and validator of my feelings since we started twelve-step programs together in the late 1980s; Sandra Tyler, my other friend who was also my champion, listener and supporter; and Ester, my cherished sister who first suggested I try twelve-step programs and validated my memories and my feelings during the most trying times of my recovery.

You all believed in me when I didn't believe in myself, and never ridiculed me or put me down for my thoughts, feelings or beliefs. You were always my cheerleaders.

I couldn't have made it without you. Thank you.

FOREWORD

PEOPLE CAN COMPLETELY HEAL from Post-Traumatic Stress Disorder (PTSD). This book is a testament to this truth. People do not have to live their lives in hopelessness, despair, depression, and self-hatred. Nor do they have to tolerate a lifetime of being tortured by past events. The human brain is a fascinating machine. It knows how to heal and has built-in healing mechanisms. But when it is overwhelmed by a hurtful event(s), it's as if a log jam is created. Little or nothing can be healed because there's too much pressure and confusion fueling the jam. The logs can't be processed through the chute and the brain has to figure out how to manage the mess. And the jam gets bigger as more hurt happens.

But that isn't the worst of it. The worst is the post-traumatic downward spiral—the impact of these unhealed "logs" long after the awful event(s) are over. It's been said that post-traumatic stress disorder is a failure of time healing our wounds. The person becomes rigid in her/his thinking and behavior, unable to create new responses appropriate to life today. It's like being locked in time internally. The person can be chronologically years past the overwhelming times but still feel and react as if these events are happening today. And to make matters harder, in its attempt to organize and manage the log jam, the brain makes incorrect beliefs about self to explain the awful events:

"I'm not lovable," "I'm not good enough," "It's my fault," "I'm powerless," "I'm not safe," "I'm a hopeless case," "I'm damaged goods," etc. And these beliefs feel true to the person and become chronic ways to define self.

The good news is people can heal their log jams. It takes time, and it requires help. I often joke with my clients that God wanted employed psychotherapists. We cannot heal from PTSD alone. If we could heal on our own, there wouldn't be the need for so many psychotherapists in this world. We cannot think well in the places where we've been hurt because of the "locked in time" phenomenon. People with PTSD need help to discharge the "log jam" of overwhelming feelings and repair the incorrect beliefs about self.

It was an honor to witness the healing described in this book. Jackie did the work; I was only a facilitator. It was my job to hold onto the truth about her "real self" until she could claim it as her own. I hate the fact that she was hurt, but I find comfort in the fact that humans are resilient and can heal from anything. It gives me great pleasure to witness the healing and watch people take their rightful place in this world—confident, self-compassionate, at peace, and thriving in their lives. This is my goal for every person I work with.

Everyone can heal and find contentment and peace. I wish this for you and all human beings.

Sincerely,

Kathy

Kathleen M. Martin, LCSW
Clinical Social Worker
Rochester, New York

SERENITY PRAYER

God grant me the serenity
To accept the things I cannot change,
The courage to
Change the things I can,
And the wisdom
To know the difference.

THE SERENITY PRAYER was a mainstay of twelve-step programs I attended for many years, and now I can say God granted me the serenity to accept the things I cannot change, the courage to change the things I can, and (usually) the wisdom to know the difference.

My heart is open; my spirit is free. I am serene, peaceful, relaxed, delighted, humorous, holy and whole, sacred and divine, and loving life! I am so blessed to have the life I have today!

I have healed my heart, and so I hope you see in my serene face all the love and joy of life I feel, even though it wasn't always that way.

The story of how I came to need the help I received in becoming free and serene no longer has much power to upset me. I include it here in case you need to recover from similar traumas or want to know the extent of trauma that can be overcome. The essence of this book lies in the pages of loving insight and affirmation that my therapist, Kathy Martin, gave me. Feel free to skip to those pages if you wish.

I was the second of five children born in the 1940s to Mr. and Mrs. Dysfunctional Rural America. As luck would have it, I was born on my father's birthday. That was the beginning of a childhood filled with neglect and physical, mental, emotional, and sexual abuse.

Fear started for me in the crib! My father was a raging alcoholic and a pedophile. When I was a baby, he worked the evening shift and came home in the middle of the night after he had stopped off at the bar. He would wake me up, sexually abuse me and put me back to bed wet and cold. He always told my mother that he got me up to keep him company while he was reading the daily paper, and she thought it was such a dear thing to do. (My grandmother even knitted me black booties so the dirt from his mechanic's job didn't show as much on my clothes.)

A neighboring teenager also raped me when I was four or five years old. This young man took me to our barn and raped me on the hay in front of the cows. He put my clothes back on as I was crying and said, "Don't tell." I didn't dare tell because I had learned from my mother that anything having to do with sex was bad and "dirty."

When I turned six, my father lost his job and we moved to a dairy farm twelve miles from any town. The house was a total shambles when we moved there; it took my parents two weeks just to get it livable enough so we could move in. We had a single cold water faucet in the kitchen sink, and my mother heated our water for cooking, bathing, and cleaning on the wood/coal cook stove. We had an outhouse and chamber pots for bathroom facilities. (I know a lot of people find chamber pots decorative, but I'm not there yet.)

Being a farmer, my father was home (raging and yelling) most of the time, and it gave him easy access to his girls. I remember being molested in barns, outhouses, fields, the silo, vehicles, a pea vinery, and the back room of our house.

I developed a fragmented psyche and post-traumatic stress disorder. Most people have heard of multiple personality disorder; this is similar, but not as extreme. Instead of one inner child, I have nine, most of them to deal with the sexual abuse and two that dealt with the rest of my life. There were so many intense feelings around the abuse that I assigned different parts of it to different fragments of my mind when I was a toddler, and when the sexual abuse became vaginal at age four or five, I created the last two fragments. They were all mind tricks, but I pictured them as children residing in different parts of my body. They seemed real to me and they kept me going.

Along with the sexual abuse, there was continual yelling by both parents, physical abuse, and ridicule. (I realize I carried the yelling into my adulthood and yelled at my children as well; they deserved better, and I was unable to give it to them.) I also was burdened by fear of my parents' disapproval; it seemed I could never do things fast enough or well enough to please them. They had a work ethic that demanded that we children be in motion all the time, except when we were sleeping or on Sunday afternoon between getting the lunch dishes washed and milking cows at five p.m. I used to love to read and was even yelled at for that—it wasn't productive enough for them.

When I was eight or nine-years old, I was taken by my father to "visit" another farmer. Little did I know Dad had another devious plan in mind. This man, I'll call him Hank, was older than my father and had grandchildren my age. He was tall and thin, had wispy, fly-away white hair and was wearing a red and blue plaid shirt. We met him across the road from his house at an old horse barn. I was very interested in the horse harnesses that were lying about and hanging on pegs on the barn's posts and beams.

While I was looking at these things, the old man took me by the hand and led me down a set of stairs to the lower part of the barn where the horse stalls used to be, and raped me. Then he dragged me back up the stairs and gave me to my father who had to carry me out to our pick-up truck. Dad left me in the truck while he and Hank loaded a piece of used farm equipment into the back of the truck—my father's payment for prostituting his daughter. After that, I couldn't walk for a day and a half and feared I had become a victim of the menacing polio epidemic of that time. I didn't realize the paralysis was from the rape and couldn't figure out why my parents didn't take me to the doctor. The other huge betrayal of the Hank incident was that before this, I felt safe with my father if others were around, but now he had taken that away from me too.

The sexual abuse by my father continued until I was almost twelve. By that time, my mind was so fragmented that I had a terrible memory and forgot things all the time. My mother hoped I would outgrow it! Eventually I did, thanks to wonderfully effective psychotherapy. I grew up, had two failed marriages and four children. I spent years in and out of depression and didn't even realize it was depression at the time. I regret that I was too emotionally ill to nurture my children properly.

I had always remembered the yelling and hollering, the ridicule and shaming, the hitting and slapping, and the rape by the family friend. However, I didn't remember the sexual abuse by my father until I was forty-eight years old (after my father had been dead three years).

In 1991 I was clinically depressed and couldn't think straight. I was having flashbacks of the childhood sexual abuse by my father, and it was disrupting my whole life. I could barely work at my real estate job and couldn't cook or work around my house. I couldn't even shop for groceries, I would go to the store, but didn't have a clue of what to buy once I got there. My husband, being extremely frustrated with my being so depressed, yelled at me about being "lazy," and the yelling brought more flashbacks of my father's continual yelling and hollering. I was a wreck!

I started seeing this wonderful therapist, Kathy Martin, LCSW, who was my lifeline for ten years and whom I continued to see until mid-2006. I saw her twice per week for most of those years, and she said many things that kept me alive and functioning during that time, words of wisdom that I still remind myself of today.

My close friend was also seeing this therapist at the same time and we were always reminding ourselves, and each other, of things Kathy had said that helped get us through our days, nights, weeks, months and years. I began writing these helpful words down, in case they could be of use to anyone else who needed words of encouragement to help them survive and, perhaps, have a better life.

Speaking of a better life! Today I live a peaceful life, day in and day out. It is an emotional level that I wasn't sure I would ever achieve. Many people my age complain that their memories aren't as sharp as they used to be, but mine is the best it has ever been. There was a picture in my therapist's waiting room that was a mosaic pattern sewn with diamond shaped pieces of colored material. The diamond shapes were in shades of red, blue, and purple. It was very pretty and it made me think of the inside of my mind, except that all of the thoughts in my mind were continually whirling around past each other in all directions all the time and I couldn't stop them enough to hang on to a thought for any length of time. What a gift to have the peaceful, quiet mind I have today.

I can (and do) think clearly and will never be depressed again. Issues continue to come into my life and the healing I did with Kathy, together with tools I learned at the Option Institute Learning and Training Center now help me work my way through them in five minutes or thirty minutes...or sometimes it takes one to two days. During the time I am working through the issue, I am peaceful and happy; I feel the old feelings and let them go and continue with my peaceful, present moment, joyful life.

I am blessed with wonderful friends with whom I can be open about how I feel, and they are open about their thoughts and feelings also. I used to be so disconnected from myself and my feelings that I didn't know how I felt, so couldn't share that with others. Consequently, I never had close relationships. I am so thankful for the relationships I have today. I have changed so many of my beliefs about what life should be like and accept whatever happens in my life now as a gift. I know that it truly is.

I was too curious to quit. I wanted to see what would happen, even if I didn't get well. Hang in there; we can get well.

I present you some of Kathy's words of wisdom that have been so helpful to me.

> "YOU MAY BE DISAPPOINTED IF YOU FAIL,
> BUT YOU ARE DOOMED IF YOU DON'T TRY."
>
> BEVERLY SILLS

Healing Places

Along my journey to wellness, I greatly appreciated
the healing power of nature. I have included
some photos of a few of my healing places.

Jackie McCullough

KATHY SAID:

How can I help you?

When I first started therapy with Kathy and was totally overwhelmed with my feelings of despair and hopelessness,

KATHY SAID:

There is a finite amount of old feelings, of old pain,

of old fear, of old anger, of old tears.

I found that hard to believe.

KATHY SAID:

It is all healable; there is an end to the old feelings.

A desperate hope that kept me going.

I would be so afraid to talk about and feel my feelings—it felt like I would literally blow apart into millions of tiny pieces—and

KATHY SAID:

The danger is over. Your feelings won't hurt you. When you were a child expressing your hurt, your parents couldn't tolerate that and they hurt you in many ways, but your feelings won't hurt you.

My life was a shambles. I couldn't focus on anything, was clinically depressed, couldn't communicate with my husband, could barely work, and felt totally hopeless to change things.

KATHY SAID:

We will get you through this.

I was glad she believed that because it sure didn't feel like it!

I was so depressed, so sad, so scared, so anxious, and could see no way out.

KATHY SAID:

You're not lost to me.

I held onto that statement for dear life for weeks, months, and years.

It felt like there was nothing but distress in my life, nothing but distress—the constant fear and anxiety. My constant companion was free-floating fear and anxiety all over my body all the time, like a second skin just under the surface of my skin. It seemed like that was who I was—this anxiety-ridden person with no moments of peace and serenity.

KATHY SAID:

You are not your distress.

I wanted to be well soon!

KATHY SAID:

*It took many years for you to get this way and it
takes a while to get better. But you will get better.*

I said: But it hurt so bad.

KATHY SAID:

I'm so sorry. What would you like me to do?

I said: Make it stop hurting.

KATHY SAID:

That's what we're doing, Sweetie.

KATHY SAID:

*Tell me how you feel. I welcome your anger. I
welcome your tears.*

I said: But when I cried my parents said,
"Nobody wants to see that ugly face!"

KATHY SAID:

They lied. You are not ugly when you cry.

When I was sure my depressed emotional state made me less of a person and couldn't believe anyone would want to spend time with me.

KATHY SAID:

You are important, you count, you matter. You matter to me and you matter to others.

I was always afraid that if I let myself feel the fear, anger, or sadness that I would get stuck in those feelings and never get out of them, but

KATHY SAID:

Feelings come and feelings go.

KATHY SAID:

Feelings won't hurt you. Your parents' behavior

and actions hurt you when you were a child, but

your feelings won't hurt you.

It really felt like they would, that my mind and
body would explode into a million pieces!!

KATHY SAID:

No, your feelings won't hurt you.

Kathy said:

You are in no danger. When you were a child there

was danger in your life; it's not like that today.

I felt so overwhelmed just talking about the sexual abuse, because I believed it wasn't okay to talk about "such things."

KATHY SAID:

Is there any danger here? Look around this room; the abuse isn't happening today. You are safe. You are safe, no matter what you talk about.

KATHY SAID:

You are safe here; there is no danger in this room.

I knew she was right, but it seemed like my father was on the other side of the door and would come bursting through at any second!

KATHY SAID:

Even if it feels that way, you are still safe here.

My parents always yelled at me for not meeting their expectations and often said: "You should be ashamed of yourself." Like the time when I was about eight and I repeated something my father had said to my uncle and I was ridiculed, for years after, for having "a big mouth." It was hard to believe I was good.

KATHY SAID:

Your goodness is a given.

KATHY SAID:

It wasn't your parents' anger that was dangerous. It was their behavior when they were angry that you were afraid of.

Today I know anger is a feeling, not a behavior. Yelling, hitting, and slapping are behaviors, not feelings.

KATHY SAID:

Your anger is not dangerous to yourself or anyone else. Your parents' behavior was what was dangerous to you when you were young.

KATHY SAID:

There is no danger here.

KATHY SAID:

You are safe.

How many times have I reminded myself of that?

(I sometimes still do.)

My family was very upset with me for disclosing the sexual abuse, and for being so depressed.

KATHY SAID:

What some other people think about your lovability does not change the fact that you are loveable.

KATHY SAID:

Remember you are good.

Oh, yes, she must believe I am good; she keeps reminding me that she believes that.

I kept forgetting about my goodness.

(I really am good?).

KATHY SAID:

Remember you are good. I will hold that belief until

you can hold it for yourself.

(She must believe it.)

(Today I believe it!)

KATHY SAID:

You are safe today; there is no one in your life who

is going to harm you.

That's right. There is no one in my life today who would hurt me. I have safe people around me.

When I was so deep down in despair and
hopelessness,

KATHY SAID:

You're not lost to me.

And I held onto that statement for dear life for
weeks and months at a time.

I found it so hard to make decisions

(I always had).

KATHY SAID:

You will know who to trust. You can trust yourself.

You can trust yourself to make appropriate

decisions for yourself.

Hard to believe, but I kept reminding myself.

My children were estranged from me.

KATHY SAID:

Remind yourself you are good.

KATHY SAID:

You want your life back!

Was that even possible?!! A life where I could put two thoughts together and put one foot in front of the other?

KATHY SAID:

It's not the feelings, (or feeling the feelings) that make us depressed, it's holding down the feelings so as not to feel them.

No WONDER I was so depressed. I was holding down a LOT of feelings!

KATHY SAID:

We will get you through this.

My husband thought I was insane and my family said I was crazy.

KATHY SAID:

You aren't crazy. Some of the behaviors of your

parents were crazy, but you aren't crazy.

Are you sure?

Yes, I'm sure, Sweetie.

I forced back the tears so as not to cry when

KATHY SAID:

Sweetie, you matter to me.

Then I learned crying was perfectly okay and very welcome and celebrated by Kathy because it is so healing.

I would often hesitate to cry because it seemed
as though if I started I would never stop.

KATHY SAID:

You have always stopped crying before. Feelings

come and feelings go. Crying is healing.

I had seen the movie *The Secret Garden* as a child. As an adult, I felt like I was totally alone and abandoned in "The Secret Garden" with big high walls all around and no gate to get out.

KATHY SAID:

Do you want to come out?

I wanted to, but could only cry; I couldn't get out.

KATHY SAID:

Do you want me to bring you a ladder so you can get over the wall?

I whispered "Yes" but I couldn't climb the ladder so...

KATHY SAID:

Shall I come and get you?

(Somebody cares.)

Another whisper: "Yes."

I pictured her coming up over the wall and down to get me (as a small child), carrying me up the ladder, over the wall and down to freedom.

KATHY SAID:

Are you out now?

I said "Yes" and sobbed and sobbed and sobbed and sobbed with profound relief! Those feelings had been locked away for so long; as bad as it felt to feel them, it was a huge relief.

I said: I miss my kids.

Kathy said:

That's so sad. They are missing so much.

Many times I thought I had slipped backward (in healing) because of the overwhelming hopelessness, distress, and discouragement.

KATHY SAID:

You can't go backward (in your healing). You are feeling these bad feelings now because your psyche wasn't ready to feel them before. You are going forward and healing all the time.

KATHY SAID:

You are good.

Repeat after me: "I am good."

KATHY SAID:

Repeat after me: "I am a good mother."

KATHY SAID:

You are a good friend.

When I didn't believe in my lovability or the value of living,

KATHY SAID:

Have you talked to God about that?

So often I felt hopeless, believing I would never be well and live peacefully.

KATHY SAID:

You are feeling hopeless today because you felt hopeless as a child and something has triggered those feelings now. Your life is not hopeless, and letting yourself feel those feelings today will reduce the reservoir of old hopeless feelings. They are just feelings, they are not reality.

When my husband believed I should be hospitalized,

KATHY SAID:

You will not have a psychotic break.

KATHY SAID:

Our pain is stored in our cells waiting to be felt and

released.

After an especially intense session, sometimes

KATHY SAID:

A few more cells know.

KATHY SAID:

Between therapy sessions you can put the pain "on a shelf" and not pay attention to it. You can be present to the moment and not pay attention to the pain.

Some days this worked and I was able to feel less fearful and depressed, and function rather normally. It took several years to do it consistently.

We were working on a memory of being at a cattle auction with my father, and him molesting me in our pickup truck on the way home. I had gone willingly, without realizing that he would molest me on the way home. I was feeling so scared and ashamed about having gone willingly.

KATHY SAID:

That was no way for a father to treat his little girl. It was his job to make you safe and not to hurt you.

I said: You mean HE was the bad one? HE was the bad one? HE was the bad one?

KATHY SAID:

You had to believe it was your fault (for going with him) because that helped you believe you had some control over your life.

Whenever I had a decision to make, I was afraid of making the "wrong" decision.

KATHY SAID:

There is no right or wrong in this. If you do "A," you will have one set of feelings, and if you do "B," you will have a different set of feelings. And that is the only difference.

KATHY SAID:

Can you promise me you won't harm yourself?

I said: No, I won't promise that.

KATHY SAID:

Can you promise you won't harm yourself before

our next session?

I said: No, I won't promise that.

KATHY SAID:

Will you promise me that if you are considering

harming yourself, you will call me first?

Yes, I will promise you that.

KATHY SAID:

Everyone has the right to initiate their own

sexuality.

One day when I arrived at Kathy's office, I hurt all over and had a splitting headache.

KATHY SAID:

Your body has stories to tell.

For several sessions in a row, I had a splitting headache.

KATHY SAID:

Thank your head for holding the pain all of these years, and remind it that the danger is over.

When I did that, the pain went away instantly. I rarely have a headache today, and when I do, I thank my head for holding the pain all of these years and remind it that the danger is over. Then the pain vanishes!

I was constantly struggling to think, to put two thoughts together.

KATHY SAID:

Your brain works perfectly fine; there is just a lot of old pain in the way right now.

_KS_

I was trying to make a decision, and kept second guessing it.

KATHY SAID:

You make good decisions for yourself.

I said: My parents said I didn't have any common sense.

KATHY SAID:

They lied.

My life had been so full of pain, betrayal, and despair.

KATHY SAID:

You just needed someone to love you.

When I said, "I just don't know how to live my life. I'll never be able to function like a normal person and have normal loving relationships."

KATHY SAID:

Who told you that?

My parents.

KATHY SAID:

They were mistaken. You are intelligent, sensitive,

humorous, caring, and loving. You aren't lost to

me.

When I was so depressed about my family relationships, and thought seriously about suicide, I asked, "What is the point of all this therapy and living, anyway, if I can't even relate to my family?"

KATHY SAID:

The world needs well people.

I guess it was enough, because I am here today and telling others the same thing when they ask, "What is the use of living?"

I was so depressed I didn't want to live.

KATHY SAID:

You are safe with me. There is no danger.

The danger is gone.

I was feeling guilty and remorseful for some mistake I had made.

KATHY SAID:

You have to learn to misbehave!

When I found I would have to spend some time at a gathering with a social worker who had done a great disservice to my children, I felt frozen, not wanting (yet needing) to go.

KATHY SAID:

You have hooked the anger and sadness of your childhood onto the anger and sadness of this present situation. That's why it seems so bad.

I could barely walk out of her office after the session was over and just sat in my car, emotionally paralyzed. After a few minutes, my head cleared and I could see the truth of what Kathy had said. I was able to go to the gathering and not be bothered by the other person.

KATHY SAID:

What are you going to do to

have fun this weekend?

Reminding me that there was fun to be had in
my life.

Kathy said I could get well, and I did! How amazing is that?

I know, and have known, so many people who have been searching for an answer to their angst in life. Some are getting better and some aren't. I can testify that there IS hope for a fear-free, anxiety-free, and depression-free life. When we feel hopeless, it is because we were hopeless as children (or during an adult trauma) and there is a trigger today that brings up the hopeless feelings from the past. The past isn't happening today, but our psyches oftentimes don't know that. When we heal the feelings from the past, those triggers no longer put us back into that child victim role; we interact in today's world as active, happy adults.

I still get triggers. Recently, I made a mistake and was embarrassed to admit it, so I checked in with a friend and did an Option Process® Dialogue (more on that later) about it. I was still holding some feelings from being seven or eight years old, when I made the mistake of throwing another child's homework away, thinking it was trash. When the teacher found it, and asked who had thrown it in there, I said I had. She called me in front of the room and told me how ashamed of me she was. I was too afraid to tell her I had thought it was trash and was just trying to be a "good girl." Then my teacher called my mother who, when I got home, also punished me for throwing the boy's homework away, and I was too afraid to tell her the reality of it because I believed she wouldn't listen to me anyway. In the dialogue session I was able to feel the feelings that I had not given myself permission to feel as a child, and heal from the incident. Now, when I think of that incident, I think of two innocent children at school; instead of seeing it with fear and pain, I see us as open, happy seven year olds who made a mistake and can laugh about it and love each other. There is such freedom in that!

At one of the twelve-step programs I used to attend, there was a saying "It's never too late to have a happy childhood." Now I really get that; we can rewrite the past—not the incidents, but our feelings about the incidents.

I started my recovery from childhood abuse in twelve-step programs. In 1989 I went to my first Al-Anon meeting and was afraid to go in, so I asked my friend, Joan, if she would like to attend an Al-Anon meeting. She agreed to go and we started our recovery together. We had both been to counselors who hadn't helped us, but Al-Anon was giving us hope. At the meetings and in the Al-Anon literature they said there is a Power greater than ourselves and we can "Let Go and Let God." Neither of us had talked about our feelings to each other (or anyone) before and now we spent hours talking about the things we were learning and about our feelings. It took me several years just to identify my feelings, because I had cut myself off from them for so long. It took me about six months to even be able to speak in the meetings.

The single most important thing that brought me to this recovery is having someone to share my struggles and hopes with, someone who completely understood what I was talking about. Joan went to Kathy before I did, and because she was getting help, I started going too. We talked for hours and hours and hours—and when some family and friends were telling us to smile and get over it, we each understood that the other couldn't just pull herself up by her bootstraps and be okay. We had been trying that for years (and sometimes succeeding) but it wasn't working in the long haul.

During my recovery, I discovered other twelve-step programs, Adult Children of Alcoholics Anonymous and Co-dependents Anonymous. Then I discovered Wayne Dyer, Deepak Chopra, Melody Beattie and The Option Institute International Learning & Training Center in Sheffield, Massachusetts, where I learned Option Process dialogues. All of these were instrumental in my healing.

I listened to the audiobook *The Seven Spiritual Laws of Success* by Deepak Chopra hundreds of times until it made more and more sense to me and parts of it became ways of life. Deepak taught a spirituality that was totally unfamiliar to me, that God is not someone "up there" judging me, and that we are all doing the best we can with our awareness and beliefs at the time. I also went to two of Deepak's seminars and I still read and listen to his books and audios today.

In 2001 I found the Option Institute. At the Option Institute, I learned that our beliefs drive all of our feelings and our responses to what is going on around us and inside us. Because I had had the therapy (and was still in therapy), I was able to take in what was being taught and took several courses there. I learned my feelings don't just happen to me, I am making them happen; that all of our feelings and actions stem from our beliefs, not from what is happening around us. I learned the Option Process® Dialogues which helped me discover what beliefs I had that were causing my distress and unhappiness. I learned how to change my beliefs by becoming aware of them and making a decision as to whether I wanted to keep the disempowering beliefs or not.

When I returned from my first one-week class at the Institute, I took a candle to my next therapy session. I handed it to Kathy, lit it, and thanked her for taking charge of my life for all of the past years of therapy. Then I took the candle from her and told her I was taking charge of my life from now on. It was a moment of such victory for both of us!

I got so much help from the Option Institute and the Option Process Dialogues, that I went on to become a certified Option Process Mentor /Counselor and now do workshops and one-on-one coaching and counseling (in person and via phone and Skype) to help others find healing and peacefulness in their lives. I find the Option Process and Option Dialogues to be the best kept secret on the planet. Most of us are not aware that we create our own feelings and they are driven by our beliefs. When we change our thinking and beliefs, we change our lives.

We can get well! We can get well!

Perhaps something here will help you. I hope so. The world can always use more well people!

And, I want you to know and remember:

YOU'RE NOT LOST TO ME.

ACKNOWLEDGMENTS

I WANT TO EXPRESS MY DEEP GRATITUDE to several people who have helped and encouraged me in the writing and publishing of this book.

First of all, Kathy Martin, LCSW. Thank you, I couldn't have gotten well or written this book without you. Joan Cook and Sandra Tyler, you were my champions and never gave up on me; and Sandra for editing my photos. Rae Foster, thank you for being my spiritual mentor these last twelve years. Phyllis LaFontaine, you listened and encouraged me to express my negative feelings as well as the positive ones and never judged me for them.

Barry and Samaria Kaufman, Beverly and Clyde Haberman of the Option Institute in Sheffield, MA, you taught me self love, authenticity, self empowerment, how to be present, and to let go of judgments. You helped me believe in myself enough to write this.

Thank you, Wendy Low, for editing my manuscript and liking it enough to want to purchase some when it is published. Ellin Veney, my niece, thank you for re-editing and giving me some valuable suggestions.

Laurie Snyder, you offered to edit and after reading it, gave few suggestions, but praised it as a useful and needed book for people who are struggling with emotional issues.

Thank you, fellow writers at Wordcrafters in Rochester, NY. Sharing my writing with you gave me more confidence to go ahead with publishing this book.

Thank you, Jeremy Sniatecki for designing the cover and logo and for valuable printing suggestions. Thank you, Nina Alvarez of Dream Your Book Auther Services, for bringing this project to fruition and to the public, and for holding my hand along the way.

I am so blessed!

ABOUT THE AUTHOR

Life Coach/Counselor **Jackie McCullough** lives and works in the Rochester, NY area. She has healed from clinical depression, a "fragmented psyche," and post-traumatic stress disorder (resulting from a childhood of violence and abuse). Jackie was certified as an Option Process® Mentor Counselor and Group Facilitator at the Option Institute in Sheffield, Massachusetts.

She uses the things she learned in psychotherapy and at the Option Institute to help others improve their lives. Advice from her therapist seemed to run through many of Jackie's conversations with other people. She often heard herself saying, "Kathy said this" or "Kathy said that." Her clients, as well as friends and associates, find these bits of wisdom helpful, and she believes others will also. She believes her most important message is: There is always hope. If she could get well, so can others.

Some of Jackie's favorite pastimes are walking in the woods, bird watching, reading, golf, yoga, meditation, and helping others triumph.

Visit her at JoyChoice.net